God's love & blessings
to you & yours'!
Mary Lou Schmidt
Sept. 9th, 2025

Miracle Butterfly Kisses from Heaven
Copyright © 2021 by Mary Lou Schmidt

Library of Congress Control Number: 2020909277
ISBN: 978-0-578-68223-5

Scripture quotations are taken from the King James Version
of the Bible.

Printed in the United States of America

Table of Contents

Dedication

I am dedicating my book to our Great God in Heaven! Also, to our precious daughter, Rachael who passed away on October 17th, 2003. For without her death, I wouldn't have my amazing miracle butterfly stories to tell.

God is the giver of life, and the taker of life! He is the one that is always in control! God dedicates His life in helping us! May we dedicate our lives in serving Him! The true living God; Father, Son and Holy Spirit!

Acknowledgment

First, I would like to thank our awesome God for giving me my amazing and beautiful miracle butterfly stories from Heaven! Your miracle butterfly stories gave me hope, comfort, and the true love of God in my heart!

Second, I would like to thank my wonderful and fantastic husband (Dick), for standing by me and supporting me in my endeavor to write this book. Thanks for being an amazing husband, and father! Also, my biggest supporter! All of his kindness and thoughtfulness will forever remain in my heart.

Thirdly, I would like to thank my sweet friend, Bonnie; for thinking of the yellow butterfly scenario for without that, we might not have our amazing butterfly stories!

Also, I would like to thank our friends and family.

To our amazing family: I could never begin to thank you all for your kind deeds, words, comfort, prayers, love, hugs and kisses during the loss of our precious daughter. Your constant love and support helped to carry us through. Family is forever! I'm so glad you're mine!

To our precious friends: Where would we be without our precious friends? Thank you so much for lifting us up and for being there when we needed you. May God richly bless you!

Finally, I would like to give a special thank you to all those who helped me in any way.

God: my never-ending praise and thanks forever!

Cory Schmidt: Thanks so much for your four fantastic butterfly and moth stories and for your awesome pictures too!

Bonnie Eskuri: Thanks for your beautiful butterfly story and pictures. I'd also like to thank you for taking that amazing picture of the sunset on October 17, 2003.

Barb Pagel: My special thanks for pushing me to get my book done! And for being my helpful spell checker.

Shelly Stringer: A special thank you to my amazing editor for helping me make my book the very best it could possibly be.

Macey Thomas: How can I ever thank you enough Macey Girl, for going above and beyond in working with me and helping to type up my book, get it printed, and published!

A special thank you to the following people for helping collect my beautiful butterfly pictures:

- Connie Majeski
- Cory Schmidt
- Sue Dyre
- Jean Stresemann
- Tristan and Raelin Schmidt
- Shirley Kellenberger

Thank you to the following people for helping collect Bible verses:

- Clint Schmidt
- Darlyn Markgraf
- Donnabell Nelson

Preface

The death of our precious daughter, Rachael Lynn Kent (Schmidt) on October 17th, 2003 prompted me to write my book. My purpose in writing this book is to glorify our great God in Heaven! God's never-ending love and mercy continued to draw us closer to Him, throughout our daughter's death. He was always there when we needed Him the most. He was with us every step of the way. Period. All we needed to do was ask. His divine compassion and love surrounded us all during our time of sadness. I would hate to think where I would be without our precious Lord to lead, guide, and direct us.

I also want to give encouragement to my readers. Life can be so much more fulfilling when you lay your burdens at the feet of Jesus! God never wants any of us to worry. He wants us to cling to Him! He is our Maker and Creator! He deserves all the praise and glory we can and should bestow upon Him! We need to help each other to Heaven, not run people down! We need to lift them up and pray for them! We need to be Godly examples – so that people will want to serve our God. Only what's done for Christ shall last! May God cover you with His feathers; and under His wings we will find refuge!

He shall cover thee with his feathers, and under his wings shalt thou trust: his truth shall be thy shield and buckler.

Psalm 91: Verse 4

God is our refuge and strength, a very present help in trouble.

Psalm 46:1

The Beginning of My Miracles!

God has blessed our lives beyond measure the past fifty-two years. God blessed us with five beautiful babies. Our family was a happy one, filled with fun, laughter, love, and lots of hugs and kisses and faith! We believed it was of uttermost importance to take our children to church as a family. We all loved going to church. The children loved and enjoyed Sunday School. They were all so intrigued by the wonderful stories of Jesus. How God sent His only begotten son, to die upon the cross and shed His blood so that we might have everlasting life. The wonderful gift of Heaven!

We were so blessed to be given the amazing gift of salvation through our precious Lord and Saviour. Repentance and conversion are the key! May we all strive to lead a Christian life and be a servant of the living God. It is such a joy, pleasure, and privilege to live a life that is pleasing to God. Don't get me wrong, we all fail miserably. Yet the Lord tells us all to strive for perfection!

I had a lot of sadness in my life when I was growing up. I was only ten when my dad died of a heart attack at age thirty-six. I was only thirty when my mom died of cancer. She was sixty. When I was forty-five, my sister died of a heart attack. My brother died too. The heaviness of loss seemed to surround me.

When Dick and I lost our daughter Rachael at age thirty-four, after an 8-year battle with cancer, we learned many things. We learned that death is never easy, no matter how old or how young. However, we learned that it made us stronger. We remembered to appreciate the little things in life and to get our priorities in order. When I started feeling sorry for myself – I needed to look around and realize there

would always be someone who has it just a little bit harder. Trust in the Lord! God is no respecter of person's!

Dick and I married and started a family. Our family and home was filled with lots of love and chaos. With four boys and a girl who liked to have fun and clown around. Darrin, Rachael, Cory, Clint, and Ben were extremely

active. They loved playing football, basketball, softball, and baseball. They also enjoyed wrestling, golf, and track.

As a young girl, Rachael enjoyed playing with her dollies and stuffed animals. She also enjoyed playing house, football and softball. She also excelled at track, cheerleading and was crowned First Princess in a Miss Winthrop Pageant. She also had fun with her dog, Tasha. Tasha was a Maltese. We all loved and enjoyed her too!

Our joyful little girl grew up to be a wonderfully positive person. Rachael was so sweet and so kind, always ready with hugs and kisses for everyone! Her beauty radiated from the inside out. She had coal black hair and dark brown eyes. Everyone loved her and her life was filled with many friends. She had the most amazing smile; she could light up a room! Rachael was a Sunday school teacher and loved the Lord!

Rachael had married a wonderful man, Darcy, who shared her love for fourteen years. I could have searched the whole world over and never found a finer son-in-law than Darcy. He is a soft-spoken, kind, honest, and loving husband and father. They quickly started their own beautiful family. Darcy and Rachael had four children. Two girls and two boys: Brooke, Macey, Tanner, and Logan.

Every year at Christmas, we would have a family get together. It was always so much fun! Eventually, as the night went on, we'd all wind up looking for Rachael. There she'd be, sitting in the middle of the room with all the little children gathered around her listening as she told them stories about Jesus! All the little children loved Rachael!

In August of 1995, our whole world turned upside down! The six-letter word, cancer, blinking and screaming at us! Our worst nightmare had come true. Our precious Rachael had cancer! How could this be? She's only 26 years old - so young! Our hearts ached inside; for her, and for all our families! Yet there wasn't anything we could do – except pray!

Prayer changes things. We always need to remember; God is the One in control! Only trust Him is one of my favorite sayings. I never asked, why my daughter, Lord? I just couldn't! I would never want to wish this on any other mother. All the grief, heartache, and tears that weighed so heavily on our hearts was almost unbearable. It was such a difficult time in all our lives. There was only one thing we could do; rely on the Lord. We always need to remember; what God does is perfect. We should never question His Wonderful Master Plan!

Rachael's youngest child Logan was only sixteen months old when she was diagnosed with breast cancer. There are many types of breast cancer and Rachael was told that her cancer was one of the top five worst. It was considered the hot kind, meaning it was very aggressive and deadly.

Our Rachael had an eight-year battle with cancer. She had thirty-four radiation treatments and six months of chemotherapy. She got her five-year clean bill of health, and three and a half months later was diagnosed with another type of cancer called Acute Lymphoblastic Leukemia (A.L.L.). It was truly a roller coaster ride!

Rachael lost her hair five times. You have no idea the frustration and devastation that she had to endure. Although, Rachael was such a trooper and never complained. We were so proud of her! She fought for another three years, but to no avail. She lost her battle to cancer on October 17th, 2003.

Rachael won her victory though. Her victory in Jesus! She was truly a shining light and example to all who knew and loved her. Blessed be her memory! Our beautiful, inside and out, princess was gone. Gone, but never-ever forgotten!

One by one their seats were emptied; one by one they went away. Now the family is parted; will it be complete one day?

Hymns of Zion songbook, #222.

We still have our precious memories to cling to. They will last us a lifetime. Just knowing she was ready and waiting for her precious Lord to take her home made our burden just a little bit lighter!

Thank you, God, for your promise of eternal life in Heaven!

Breathtakingly Beautiful Sunset

Photo was taken at 5:15 pm, on October 17th, 2003, at the time of Rachael's death.

For my yoke is easy, and my burden is light.

Matthew 11:30

My Miracle Butterfly Promise!

On December 10th, 2002 Rachael had a meeting with her oncologist. Our whole family was there to support her. She was told she had only two or three months to live. "Take one last trip as a family, and get your house in order," they said. A sad day was had by all!

Darcy, Rachael, and their sweet family decided to go to Hawaii for two weeks. The kids were so excited they could hardly wait. Vacations are always so much fun. I took them to the airport. The kids looked so cute pushing their own luggage on wheels.

When they returned home everyone said, "Hawaii was awesome!" They had a big beautiful Hawaiian flower centerpiece on their table from Rachael's cancer doctor when they arrived. You seldom ever hear of that! They were so surprised, and the Hawaiian flower arrangement was so huge and so beautiful! Rachael started to cry. "My oncologist is so special," she said. "I just love him so much!"

They took lots of pictures while on vacation and had a good time! About seven months later, she called me.

"Mom," she said, "could you and Bonnie come over to my house and put my Hawaiian pictures into picture books?"

"Of course I will, princess," I answered. "Line it up with Bonnie (one of her best friends), and I'll take some vacation from work."

The following week we got together to do her books! I suggested that we get a system going. "Rachael, pick a book, and then pick the first ten pictures you'd like to start with," I said. I gave Bonnie the book and took the ten pictures from Rachael and handed them to Bonnie one at a time. Then I would grab another ten pictures, and Bonnie would slide them into her book. It really went slick. We finished the first photo book. Bonnie began filling the second book too. We were about half done with the second book, when I handed Bonnie a picture of Rachael with a Hawaiian flower in her hair.

Bonnie glanced down at the picture and began to cry. "I'm so sorry, Rachael," said Bonnie. "Here you lay dying, and I'm feeling sad for myself that God is taking you out of my life!" Rachael reached up and grabbed Bonnie's forearm. "It's alright Bonnie, don't cry," said Rachael. "God will take care of you just as He has taken care of me for the past eight years! I know He will," said Rachael!

Bonnie looked at Rachael with tears streaming down her face. "Rachael," Bonnie said; "when you pass on, I want you to come to me on my worst days in the form of a yellow butterfly! (She fluttered her fingers together three times).

I looked at Bonnie, and then I looked at Rachael. "Me too, me too," I said. "Yellow butterfly, white butterfly, monarch butterfly - I don't care, me too!" I put my hands over Rachael's and began to squeeze them. She just shrugged her shoulders.

I proceeded to put my hands over Rachael's a second time! "Rachael honey," I said; "no one knows what Heaven will be like. You will if you can, right? You will if you can?"

"Of course, I will, Mom," she said. "I will if I can!" Rachael shook her head yes and we all started to cry again!

Bonnie jumped off the bed to get a box of Kleenex for all of us. We continued to finish the other photobooks. After an hour or two, Bonnie and I left to go home. Nothing more was said.

Three and a half weeks after Rachael promised to come back to us in the form of a butterfly, our precious angel became bed ridden. We had Rachael propped in bed. The hospice nurse told us to knock before we entered her room - so she wouldn't get scared. Every once in a while, I would knock and peek into her room. She would just smile and tap on the bed.

"Come sit, or come lay by me, Mom!" She would always say with enthusiasm; so, I would. I laid beside her on the bed, and we were talking – it was about 2:30 pm on Friday. Suddenly, Rachael whispers to me, "Mom, do you hear that?" I listened for a minute, but I couldn't hear anything.

"Shh," Rachael said again; "Do you hear the beautiful singing?"

"No, I can't," I replied.

"Mom, the singing is so beautiful; can you really not hear it?"

"No, I honestly can't, that's only for you princess," I said, with tears streaming down my face.

"It's time," she said. "Go, get Darcy and the kids." Rachael passed away on October 17th, 2003 at 5:15 pm.

I called Bonnie; she instantly ran outside to check the sunset. She said it was absolutely amazing! The sky was breathtakingly beautiful! It was by far the most beautiful sunset I have ever seen! Praise be to God! He was waiting for her.

Our whole world came shattering down before us. We had over eight years to say good-bye, but it still wasn't enough. Our precious angel was gone! Gone, but never forgotten!

Unless you have experienced the loss of a child; you have no clue about all the emotions you go through. All of the heartache, grief, frustration, devastation, and sadness that overcame me was almost unbearable. I felt like someone reached into my chest and yanked a piece right out of my heart and I knew I would never be the same.

However, faith always sees us through! We must take our burdens to the Lord and lay them at the feet of Jesus! God will take care of us!

Little did I know, that over the next fifteen years that God would bless me with thirteen miracle butterfly stories!

God's true compassion and love for us never ceases to amaze me! Thank you, Lord, for the divine comfort, mercy, and reassurance that you so graciously bestowed unto us! Dick and I will praise and glorify Your High and Holy Name until our last breath! I will love and cherish my miracle butterfly stories forever!

Canvas painting by Raelin Schmidt

Blessed are they that mourn: for they shall be comforted.

Matthew 5:4

Chapter 1
The Funeral Miracle!

Rachael received ninety-eight flower arrangements, angels, plaques, etc. at her visitation and over 1,000 people attended. We had a steady line of people from 3:20 pm until 9:45 pm, non-stop. We were all exhausted, to say the least.

I received my first miracle butterfly story on the day of Rachael's funeral, October 21st, 2003. 749 people attended her funeral! The church was packed with people! Right before Rachael's funeral started, an usher opened a window in front of the church. Beautiful rays of sunshine filled the room, especially the pulpit area. Everyone gasped, oh! You could just feel the power of God in the room! It was so amazing!

The minister preached about Rachael being a runner. Rachael loved to run; she loved how her body felt when she was finished. She would try to run at least three to five miles every day. "It's quite a rush, Mom," she would say! Rachael and her brother, Darrin, ran a 27-mile marathon! That was on her bucket list.

The minister began his sermon on the importance of running the race; the Christian's race. The only race that really matters, is the race that is run for Christ! It's the race that is run for Christ! We all need to be a shining light, an example for all to follow! "We all knew where Rachael stood on her beliefs," stated the minister.

Darcy and Rachael taught their children the importance of going to church and Sunday School. They also taught them how important it was to say their prayers every night. She would tell them to be kind, loving, and respectful individuals. Always love the Lord, she would tell them.

The church was filled to capacity! Wow! What a wonderful tribute to her! Rachael lost her battle to cancer, but she won her victory in Jesus! May we all strive to win our victory too!

After the funeral, we all went over to Darcy and Rachael's house. We stayed there until 4:15 pm. We changed clothes and proceeded to go home. When we got home, I had Dick park our car in the driveway. That way we could access the trunk and doors easily. There were plants and flowers everywhere! The whole backseat, floor, and trunk were full of flower arrangements and plants. Plus, I had one big plant on the floor in the front seat; and I was also holding one on my lap.

As Dick unlocked the door to our home, I grabbed two pots of flowers from our car and carried them into our kitchen. I set them on the counter and went back for two more. Dick was also carrying pots of flowers to the house. As I grabbed another two pots from the car, I felt something touch the calf of my left leg. When I lifted my right leg to shoo it away, it touched my left leg again. With the pots still in my hands, I bent over to see what it was. It was the biggest, brightest yellow butterfly I'd ever seen! It was weaving in and out of my legs, like a figure eight! I just stood there amazed and crying!

I instantly thought of Rachael's promise to Bonnie and me, "I will if I can, Mom. I will if I can!"

For God so loved the world, that he gave his only begotten son, that whosever believeth in him should not perish, but have everlasting life.

John 3:16

Chapter 2

The Miracle at Rachael's Gravesite!

I received my second miracle butterfly story in Fall 2003. Darcy and the kids would always decorate Rachael's grave. They would put long-stemmed red roses all the way around the grave site. They put four decorated pumpkins down the middle and fresh flowers throughout the rest.

On November 1st, 2003, our son Clint and his wife, Magdalena went to Rachael's grave site to see it because they hadn't been there since she died. They had asked us to go with them, but we couldn't go that Sunday after church. When they arrived, they said the grave plot was breathtakingly beautiful! "What an amazing sight!" they exclaimed. They said they just stood there and cried.

However, we didn't get to the grave site until November 16th. It was the first time Dick and I went to the cemetery after Rachael's death and everything was frozen and mostly covered with snow. On this cold November day is when I was blessed with my second miracle butterfly story.

A sadness washed over me as Dick, and I walked hand in hand to the gravesite. I began, "Hi princess, it's just Mom and Dad, we love you!" We both started to cry. Our sweet princess was gone! Oh, how we missed her! Our hearts ached with grief! We were happy for Rachael – yet sad she was gone. It was so bittersweet!

As we stood there, I looked up at the sky; and I began to pray out loud. I stood with my feet apart and with my hands folded against my chest.

"Thank you, God, for giving us such an awesome and amazing daughter! She was so beautiful, inside and out. She was so special! She was kind, loving, and thoughtful and she loved you, Lord! I always wondered why you only gave us one daughter; but then realized no other daughter could ever compare to Rachael!"

When I was praying, the wind started to blow. It kept getting stronger.

"I promise you Lord; we will never turn bitter! We will always praise and glorify Your High and Holy Name!" I no sooner got the words out of my mouth; when a huge gust of wind swirled twice in front of me and blew right into my face! It felt as though someone shoved a two-hundred mile an hour fan right in my face! I kept gasping for air and backing up at the same time. Finally, I gasped one last time. My husband leaped towards me, "are you alright?" he asked. I began nodding my head yes, and said, "oh truly, Lord, thou art our All-Mighty, All-Powerful, and Omnipotent God!" Dick just stared at me in amazement!

"I have to finish my prayer," I said, while looking up at the sky. When I was done praying, I laid my face into my hands and began to cry.

After I regained my composure, Dick and I just stood there staring at the frozen flowers and pumpkins. It wasn't very long - when suddenly a light yellow butterfly flew up out of the frozen flowers! It flew up, swirled twice, and then touched the ground three times.

"Look, look," I said, "it's a butterfly!" Tears were streaming down my face. Within seconds, it started to swirl all over us again! It flew to my left side, swirling twice. Then it flew around to the back of me, swirling twice. Then it flew to my right side, swirling twice. Finally, it just fluttered beside me! It was so close to me I could've touched the nose of the butterfly with my index finger. Dick and I just stood there. What had just transpired before our very eyes? God's divine comfort!

I thought of Rachael's promise, "I will if I can!"

Surely goodness and mercy shall follow me all the days of my life: and I will dwell in the house of the Lord for ever.

Psalm 23:6

Chapter 3

My Kitchen Window Miracle!

I received my third miracle butterfly story in the summer of 2004. It was a Friday. I had spent all morning cleaning my house. I was so sad that day. I was dusting every picture and each time, I picked up one of Rachael, it would make me well up with tears!

About noon, I came into the kitchen to make myself a little individual pizza. I put it in the microwave and sat down to pray. When I had finished my prayer, my heart was so sad! I got up from the table and took the pizza out of the microwave. I sat back down at the table and started to eat. I was almost done eating, when I happened to glance at Rachael's picture on the counter smiling at me. I laid my face into my hands and began to cry. I started sobbing uncontrollably. My body was shaking!

Suddenly, I heard a little noise. I wiped the tears off my eyes and looked to the right. There was a bright yellow butterfly tapping on my window! It tapped four times, and then another four times. As if to say; "it's O.K. Mom, it's O.K. Mom, please don't cry!" It continued to tap all over my window! I could hardly believe my eyes!

I thought of our sweet daughter's promise, "I will if I can!"

For I am persuaded, that neither death, nor life, nor angels, nor principalities, nor powers, nor things present, nor things to come, Nor height, nor depth, nor any other creature, shall be able to separate us from the love of God, which is in Christ Jesus our Lord.

Romans 8:38-39

Chapter 4

The Boat Miracle at Diamond Lake!

I received my fourth miracle butterfly story on August 22nd, 2005, Rachael's Birthday.

In June of 2005, our special friends, Bruce and Audrey, called and asked if we would consider going with them on a fishing trip. "Maybe we could go to Cory and Clint's cabin on Diamond Lake? Of course, we'll pay them," Audrey said. Our two sons owned a cabin on Diamond Lake.

"Sure, let's go! That sounds like so much fun!" I said. We decided to go the week of August 21st, 2005. Bruce and Audrey picked us up after church on Sunday. When we got to the cabin, we unloaded everything and put it all away. We were all hungry, so Audrey and I made something to eat for us. It was starting to get late, so we decided to dock the boat in the morning.

When Dick and I awoke the next morning, I hugged him and asked if he remembered that it was Rachael's birthday.

"No, I didn't." he replied. We embraced again, and just stood there for a while.

We all decided we wanted to go fishing. Audrey and I made breakfast while Dick and Bruce docked the boat. We were the only boat on the lake. Dick was at the front of the boat, Bruce was on the left side, Audrey was on the right, and I was in the back of the boat. It was about 10:30 in the morning. We were still fishing in the middle of the lake.

As we sat there fishing, I looked out at the lake water and up at the sky thinking about what a beautiful day it was. What a beautiful day to have a birthday! I started silently talking to Rachael who was on my mind.

"Happy Birthday, Princess, wherever you are! I love you! I didn't forget! I know you're out there somewhere! Happy Birthday, Rachael!"

Then I got an idea. I touched Audrey's forearm with the back of my hand.

"Audrey, it's Rachael's birthday today. I'm going to count to three. Let's holler as loud as we can, 'Happy Birthday, Rachael, we love you!'" I said.

"Okay, let's do it," she said.

"Tell Dick and Bruce," I replied.

"Okay Mary Lou, go ahead," Audrey stated.

I held up my hand and began to count, "One, two, three!"

"Happy Birthday, Rachael! We love you!" We all hollered.

Ten to twenty seconds later, a big orange and black monarch butterfly appeared swirling over the top of our boat in the middle of the lake! We all started to cry.

"Mary Lou, I can't believe how God blesses you with these miracle butterfly stories," said Audrey.

I instantly thought of Rachael's promise, "I will if I can!"

Therefore if any man be in Christ, he is a new creature: old things are passed away; behold, all things are become new.

2 Corinthians 5:17

Chapter 5
The Deer Hunting Miracle!

I received my fifth miracle butterfly story on Saturday November 12th, 2005. Deer hunting on Darrin's land was always a tradition! Our whole family loved to go and so did Rachael. I would make two big pots of homemade chili, a jellyroll pan of homemade Special-K bars, a jellyroll pan of homemade brownies with homemade fudge frosting, and chocolate chip cookies, if I'd have time. We ate good! Yummm!

I was sitting at my deer stand. Our boys had built a boxed deer stand for me, with a door and a 6'x8' platform. They built about thirteen to fifteen wooden steps to get to the enclosed platform. I was so lucky to have such a nice stand.

It was such a nice day. The sun was out. I was sitting outside on the platform of my deer stand with all my hunting gear on, and I began to sweat. I took off my hunting jacket and laid it on the platform. I kept looking around for any movement. When out of nowhere, a beautiful bright yellow butterfly appeared and landed on my left forearm! I just sat there staring at the pretty butterfly! With tears streaming down my face, I looked up to Heaven and gave thanks to Him (God) for His unbelievable love and mercy!

I thought of Rachael's promise, "I will if I can!"

But Jesus said, Suffer little children, and forbid them not, to come unto me: for of such is the kingdom of heaven.

Matthew 19:14

Chapter 6

The Jesus Loves Me Singing Miracle!

I received my sixth miracle butterfly story on Tuesday, August 22nd, 2006, Rachael's birthday.

Every year I have a special week that I call Grandma's Week! It just so happened that August 21st, 2006 was the start of Grandma's Week for my little grand girlies: Bryce, Kala, Regan and Sierra!

They arrived at our house around noon on Monday. I remember taking the girls swimming that day. We played lots of games. BINGO for prizes was their favorite. They had a blast.

Before long, it was bedtime. I tucked them all into their sleeping bags. They all said their prayers. I hugged and kissed them all goodnight They were all snuggled in – and happy to be at G-ma's house! I absolutely love my grandchildren! My grandchildren melt my heart!

Tuesday morning, I got up early and made them all breakfast. They love my French toast and sausages. I told them we needed to get the dishes done first, and then I'd have a special surprise for them. After the dishes were done, I took the grand girlies outside to our front lawn. I told them it was Auntie Rachael's birthday up in Heaven, and we were going to sing happy birthday to her. We formed a big circle, and all joined hands. The little girlies sang their hearts out!

After we finished singing, our granddaughter Sierra walked over to me and tugged on my top.

"Grandma," she said; "maybe Jesus would like it if we sang 'Jesus Loves Me', too!"

"That's a great idea, Sierra. Girlies, girlies, let's make our big circle again. We're going to sing Jesus Loves Me," I said.

We sang the first verse. As we sang the second verse, a big black, orange, brown and white monarch butterfly came out of nowhere and began swirling over the top of our circle. I pulled my camera off my wrist and began taking pictures of our miracle butterfly!

It flew all over our front lawn! It was so exciting to see!

I started to cry as I thought of Rachael's promise to us, "I will if I can!"

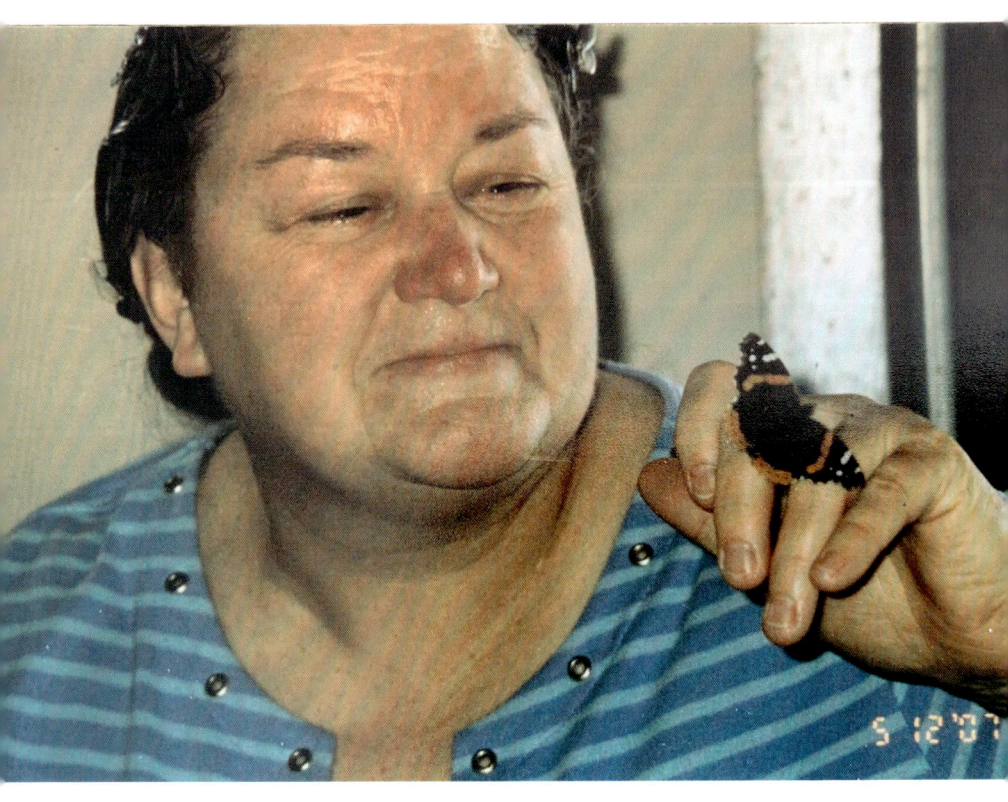

But thanks be to God, which giveth us the victory through our Lord Jesus Christ. Therefore, my beloved brethren, be ye stedfast, unmoveable, always abounding in the work of the Lord, forasmuch as ye know that your labour is not in vain in the Lord.

1 Corinthians 15:57-58

Chapter 7
The Amazing Miracle in My Garage!

I received my seventh miracle butterfly story on Saturday, May 12th, 2007. It was the Saturday before Mother's Day. It was also the first day of the fishing opener. It was around three o'clock in the afternoon and I had been cleaning all day. I came up from the basement and plopped on the couch. I was tired from the day's work. I rested my head on the back of the sofa and closed my eyes for a bit.

Out of the blue, I heard a voice. The voice said to me, "take the garbage out." I looked up, that's the only thing I hadn't done yet. "No, I'm not." About a minute or two later, the voice came to me again, only louder. "Take the garbage out!"

"No, I'm not going to take the garbage out," I said to myself. The voice came to me a third time, even louder yet, "Take the garbage out.". I instantly thought of the doubting Thomas. "Okay Lord, I'll take the garbage out," I said as I looked at my living room ceiling. I quickly jumped off the couch and started to collect all the garbage. As I tied the tall kitchen bag shut, I slid into my shoes and proceeded to take the garbage out. As I walked out to the garage and reached for the garage door handle, something flew by my head and startled me. When I looked, I noticed it was a pretty red admiral butterfly!

It landed on the ledge of the garage door, where the windowpane and the wood meet in the middle. It was a beautiful red, brown, white, and orange butterfly (not a monarch). I quickly pulled my hand back from the garage door handle. I took about four steps backwards and sat on my steps in the garage - watching the beautiful butterfly.

After watching it on the window for quite some time, I had an idea! I needed my camera. I went into the house to find it, but I couldn't. Then I remembered I had left it in my car. I opened the car door quietly; I didn't want to scare the butterfly away. I got the camera out of the car and began taking pictures.

I thought of my girlfriend, Jean Stresemann. I had told her some of my butterfly stories before. I called Jean and told her about the pretty butterfly on my garage door.

"I'm coming over," she said.

"Okay," I said, "but please go to the backdoor of the garage so you won't scare the butterfly away."

It wasn't long and here she was. I took her to the front garage door and showed her the butterfly. She could hardly believe it.

"Oh my, it's so pretty," said Jean. I told her I had taken some pictures of it.

"Go get your camera, I'll take some pictures of you with the butterfly," she said. I handed her the camera.

"Talk to the butterfly like it's your daughter," said Jean. I shook my head no and she said, "do it! Put your hand on the door and talk to her."

I glanced up at her again, and she said, "get going!" With tears streaming down my face, I began talking to the pretty butterfly with my hand pressed against the door.

"It's your Mama," I said. "I loved you then, I love you now, and I will love you forever and always, Rachael!"

As soon as I said that, the butterfly still positioned on the far-right side of the door pivoted to the left and began walking toward my hand.

"Oh, Mary Lou, it's going to crawl on your hand," said Jean.

"I think so," I replied. We were both crying. It did! It crawled onto my hand and up my index finger. I lifted my hand off the door and Jean took some pictures. Did this just happen? We could hardly believe it!

Just then, my daughter-in-law, Magdalena, and granddaughters, Sierra, and Cheyenne Mary, showed up at our house. Go to the back door!

When my granddaughter, Sierra, saw the butterfly on my hand, she instantly wanted to hold it.

"No," I said. I knew that wasn't the right attitude, so I quickly changed my mind.

"Give me your hand," I said. We put our hands side by side and I slid the butterfly onto her hand. The butterfly pivoted and walked right back onto my hand!

"Why won't the butterfly stay on my hand?" asked Sierra.

"I don't know," I said. We tried two more times, but the butterfly would always crawl back onto my hand! Sierra didn't understand.

"That's because God sent this Miracle Butterfly for your Grandma," said Jean. I put my hand on the front garage door again. I slid the butterfly onto the door, and it didn't move. It just sat there. We stood there in amazement!

Dick and Clint came home from fishing around 9:00 pm. We showed them the pretty butterfly on the garage door. I told them the story of my miracle butterfly and how she appeared on my door about 3:20 that afternoon. We couldn't believe it was almost 9:30 at night and she was still there!

"Do you think we should let the butterfly go now?" asked Clint. I shook my head yes. Clint told me to open the electric garage door and I did.

The butterfly flew up, swirled twice, touched the garage door again, and then flew out! It was a red admiral butterfly!

The next day was Mother's Day!

I thought of Rachael's promise to us, "I will if I can!"

But the Comforter, which is the Holy Ghost, whom the Father will send in my name, he shall teach you all things, and bring all things to your remembrance, whatsoever I have said unto you.

John 14:26

Chapter 8
The Beauty Shop Miracle!

I received my eighth miracle butterfly story on June 21st, 2008. It was my sixty-first birthday!

I wanted to get my hair washed, so I made an appointment at the salon for Saturday morning, June 21st.

When I was leaving Tammy's Beauty Shop, I thought of Rachael and how she used to call me on my birthday every year.

"Happy Birthday, Mom," she would say. "I love you!"

Thinking of those memories, I started to cry.

By this time, I was at my car unlocking the door. Something flew past my head. I got into my car and started it. When I looked up, there was a bright yellow butterfly tapping on my car and windows!

I thought of Rachael's promise, "I will if I can!"

Grace be unto you, and peace, from God our Father, and from the Lord Jesus Christ. I thank my God always on your behalf, for the grace of God which is given you by Jesus Christ;

1 Corinthians 1:3-4

Chapter 9
The Traveling Miracle!

I received my ninth miracle butterfly story on June 21st, 2011.

On June 20, 2011, I went to New Ulm to join Anytime Fitness. The next day, on my birthday, I went to New Ulm to work out. When I was leaving, I started to think about Rachael. Oh, how I miss you, Rachael! I thought to myself. I started to cry. My heart was so sad!

As I rounded the last corner, before I went up the hill to go home, butterflies came out of nowhere. I bet I had at least fifty to sixty butterflies tap and touch my car and windows for the whole 19-mile drive home!

I thought of Rachael's promise, "I will if I can!"

But if we walk in the light, as he is in the light, we have fellowship one with another, and the blood of Jesus Christ his Son cleanseth us from all sin.

1 John 1:7

Chapter 10
The Miniature Golf Miracle!

I received my tenth miracle butterfly story in August of 2014. I was having Grandma's Week for my two grandsons, Luke and Tristan.

We went to Hutchinson to play miniature golf. While we were playing, a beautiful black, yellow and orange butterfly appeared. It followed us from hole to hole. We all laughed and shook our heads. We could hardly believe it! It would not leave us alone! I bet it followed us for five or six holes. It swirled from side to side and all around us! It encircled each one of us, time after time! It was amazing!

I thought of Rachael's promise, "I will if I can!"

Let not your heart be troubled: ye believe in God, believe also in me. In my Father's house are many mansions: if it were not so, I would have told you. I go to prepare a place for you.

John 14: 1-2

Chapter 11
The Patio Miracle!

I received my eleventh miracle butterfly story in the Fall of 2014.

I was in the kitchen doing dishes at the sink. I happened to look outside and noticed lots of butterflies flying all over my backyard! I was intrigued, so I stepped out onto our patio. Our neighbor's three bushes were covered with monarch butterflies. I left the patio and walked over to the neighbor's bushes. There were hundreds of monarch butterflies. I couldn't believe my eyes! What a sight to behold! I stood there for quite some time. The butterflies were so beautiful! Intrigued by their beauty and numbers, I watched their every movement!

As I turned to go back on my patio; a big bright orange, black, and white monarch butterfly kept swirling around me. It followed me back onto my patio. It encircled me, and then proceeded to swirl and fly all over our patio and deck!

Suddenly the butterfly swirled side to side and then landed on top of one of the post-caps on my patio railing! I started to cry. It stayed there for a while, and then flew away. It was definitely another sign of God's divine love and comfort!

I immediately thought of Rachael's promise to Bonnie and me, "I will if I can!"

Thy word is a lamp unto my feet, and a light unto my path.

Psalm 119:105

Chapter 12
Clint's Car Miracle!

I received my twelfth miracle butterfly story on Sunday, July 10th, 2016.

Dick and I went to Illinois for our nephew's baptism.

Clay was so happy to see us. We stayed for the meal they had prepared for the company. After church was over, there was quite a line of cars waiting to leave. We hurried to get in line. Our son, Clint, and his family were waiting in line too. We motioned for Clint to go ahead of us. As they pulled ahead of us, a big bright yellow butterfly appeared out of nowhere touching and tapping all over their car! It was amazing to watch!

I thought of Rachael's promise, "I will if I can!"

For by grace are ye saved through faith; and that not of yourselves: it is the gift of God: Not of works, lest any man should boast.

Ephesians 2: 8-9

Chapter 13
The Mother's Day Miracle!

I received my thirteenth miracle butterfly story on Mother's Day, May 13th, 2018.

Our son, Darrin, had invited us to spend a couple of days with them to celebrate Mother's Day Weekend.

Darrin and Jackie took us out for dinner on Friday night. It was my Mother's Day present. On Saturday, Darrin and Jackie invited some other friends to join us for a delicious meal. We played some games and had a great time!

We left Darrin's about six o'clock on Sunday morning. We were halfway home, when I started to think of our sweet, Rachael. I missed her so! Gone, but never forgotten! I started to cry. I thought of her sweet husband Darcy and how amazing and wonderful he had been helping her through her battle with cancer. Her children too; Brooke, Macey, Tanner and Logan. They all tried to help the best they could by doing the dishes, cleaning up, and doing as they were told. My heart just ached!

Life isn't easy when you have only one parent. As I was wiping the tears from my eyes, I glanced up and a beautiful bright orange butterfly flew across our front truck window.

I thought of Rachael's promise, "I will if I can!"

I had fainted, unless I had believed to see the goodness of the Lord in the land of the living. Wait on the Lord: be of good courage, and he shall strengthen thine heart: wait, I say, on the Lord.

Psalm 27:13-14

Chapter 14

Cory's Twin Butterfly Miracle!

My first Miracle Butterfly story occurred in Summer 2006 on Diamond Lake, which is near Spicer, Minnesota.

We were spending the weekend at our cabin. One morning I decided to head out walleye fishing before sunrise.

As the sun started to rise, I caught a walleye on my hook! I instantly took the fish off my line and threw it in my live well. I glanced up just in time to see two beautiful monarch butterflies descend upon my boat!

I sat there in awe! They were orange, yellow, black, and white. I can't begin to explain all the joy, peace and excitement I felt!

They decided to fish with me for twenty minutes! I know Rachael was with me because she loved going to Diamond Lake!

These things I have spoken unto you, that in me ye might have peace. In the world ye shall have tribulation: but be of good cheer; I have overcome the world.

St. John 16:33

Chapter 15
Cory's Luna Moth Miracle!

My second Miracle Butterfly story happened in June 2009.

After returning home from a long, hard and stressful day at work, I walked into my garage and noticed a beautiful green Luna moth inside. A Luna moth only lives for fourteen days! It was absolutely stunning! As I approached it, it flew off the wall and landed on my right arm. I instantly thought of Rachael! What an amazing sight!

I went running into the kitchen of our home and told my beautiful family. We all rushed back to the garage. It was still there. What a beautiful sight to behold!

It landed on each of us and circled all around us! It was so awesome! We were all so excited and amazed that we cried, and we were filled with such joy! We could definitely feel Rachael's presence among us. It touched all our hearts!

After about a half an hour, we decided to set the Luna Moth free. Wow, what a fantastic experience!

Blessed be God, even the Father of our Lord Jesus Christ, the Father of mercies, and the God of all comfort.

2 Corinthians 1:3

Chapter 16

Cory's Pontoon Miracle!

My third Miracle Butterfly story occurred on June 26th, 2019.

Our family decided to go to Nashville to celebrate the 21st birthday of our sweet daughter, Kala Rachael.

On the third day in Nashville, we decided to take an hour and a half trip west. We rented a pontoon to go fishing and boating. We had twenty-eight miles of river to travel.

Our second stop was at a feeder creek. We went fishing and swam. As we were getting ready to leave and go farther up the river, a beautiful black butterfly with tiny white spots landed on my son, Gage! The butterfly took turns landing on all of us! First Gage, then Nikki, Bryce, Kala, and Regan!

As we departed, I was sitting on the slide of the second deck. Suddenly, the butterfly left Regan and landed on my right shoulder. I started to cry. The butterfly didn't leave my shoulder for twenty minutes!

Once again, we felt our sweet Rachael's presence! It was breathtaking!

Let your conversation be without covetousness; and be content with such things as ye have: for he hath said, I will never leave thee, nor forsake thee.

Hebrews 13:5

Chapter 17
Cory's Circle Miracle!

My fourth miracle butterfly story happened in the Summer of 2019. I was visiting my cousin, Matt Schmidt.

It was 8:12 pm in the evening on July 18th, 2019. As I took my ladder out of my truck and started to set it up, a red admiral butterfly landed on my head. It startled me!

There were five guys standing around in a circle, but the butterfly landed on my head.

"Give me your phone so I can take your picture," said Matt.

Matt took two pictures as we stood there gazing at the beautiful butterfly! Matt made a comment, "We all know who is with us!"

I was so excited to show my Mom the pictures of my miracle butterfly encounter! Wow!

Know ye not that they which run in a race run all, but one receiveth the prize? So run, that ye may obtain.

1 Corinthians Chapter 9: Verse 24

Chapter 18

Bonnie's Running Miracle!

It was the summer of 2004, and I was having an especially rough day. I was missing Rachael so much! I just needed to get out and run. Rachael and I both loved running.

I went to see Rachael at Fairview Hospital one day. When we were sitting in her room looking out the window, we saw many people outside running. Rachael said she really missed being able to run. I asked if it bothered her to watch them run. Because Rachael was so special, she of course answered, "No, it makes me so happy for them!" That day she told me to run for her, and so I did. She was always with me on my runs.

Rachael and I had such a special friendship! We had so much in common and could relate to each other so well. She was my very best friend!

She was the friend who walked beside me down a busy street in the middle of the afternoon, holding my hand. (We got a lot of looks and honks.) She was the friend I loved to shop with, go out to eat with, and talk to on the phone for hours; even if it was two in the morning! We laughed together, cried together, and just enjoyed being together!

Rachael had a way of making everyone happy. She was the most beautiful person, inside and out. So, it was no wonder I would carry her with me on my runs.

On a hot summer day in 2004, I laced up my tennis shoes to go out for a run. As I was running, I started to cry. I struggled to keep running. Every thought was of Rachael. It wasn't long, and I was crying so hard I could barely breathe. I found myself talking out loud to her; telling her how much I missed her and needed her in my life! At that very moment, the most beautiful monarch butterfly swirled out in front of me. It swirled and fluttered around me like crazy. It flew next to me for a few seconds as I ran. I sobbed even harder then, because I knew it was Rachael. She was telling me that everything was going to be okay. Just then, a peaceful feeling came over me. I softly whispered, "I love you, Rachael!"

Epilogue

A special letter to my readers!

In October of 2017, I had such an unusual feeling come over me! I had such a joy in my heart; yet my heart was so heavy! I felt so unworthy!

What had I done to deserve to be treated so special from God?

My mind kept dwelling on the past thirteen years then the fourteenth, and so on. Miracle after miracle butterfly encounters! They were all so special and so heartwarming!

My heart was so overwhelmed with gratitude and thankfulness to God! He continued to bless me year after year! Now it was my turn. What could I do for you Lord? I am your servant, please show me Lord!

I walked out onto our patio deck. It was such a gorgeous night, with a full moon and lots of stars! How gracious and good God had been to me and to our whole family! It was almost unbelievable! Such love and compassion from God! I could hardly keep my composure!

I looked up at the sky and started talking out loud to the Lord. "I am so thankful and grateful God; how can I ever repay you?" "What can I do to bless you, Lord?" I started to cry!

That night when I went to bed, I had a dream! The Lord told me in my dream to write a book. What better choice than His amazing miracle butterfly encounters He gave unto me!

I promised the Lord the next day that I would write Him a special book to glorify His High and Holy name!

After two years, I finally finished your book, Lord! Just in time for Thanksgiving of 2019. I can wake up Thanksgiving Day and kneel by my bed and say, "Your book is done, Lord!"

Farewell to my Readers!

I would personally like to express my sincere thanks and gratitude to all those who purchased my book. Life is so fragile, handle it with prayer! I pray God will touch your hearts and lives in some special way, too! He touched our lives, and we have never been the same!

Cling to Jesus, He is your Saviour and King! Reach out to the Lord and to your precious loved ones when you are in need. He is always there to help us – all we need to do is ask!

My miracle butterfly encounters are proof there is a God in Heaven! God deserves all the praise, honor and glory that is due Him! It gave me great joy to write my book and dedicate it to God and Rachael! Blessed be her memory. May God bless each of you beyond measure!

My Sincere Thanks,
Mary Lou Schmidt